Internal Branding:

A How-To Guide

by

Nina MacLaverty
&
Hugh Oddie

Copyright

Internal Branding: a How-To Guide

Copyright © 2015 by Nina MacLaverty & Hugh Oddie

Dedication

This book is a practical, concise "how-to" for Internal Branding. It will appeal to all levels of employees, from the most senior officers down. It is dedicated to all those who understand and believe in the power of branding as a major driver of business success and because they will understand that:

- ➢ Companies which have a strong internal brand are more profitable and successful

- ➢ Employees are crucial in delivering the required customer experience, which is dependent on the effectiveness of the Internal Branding programme

- ➢ An Internal Branding programme literally acts as the bridge between business strategy and implementation.

An effective Internal Branding Programme enriches people's lives.

Acknowledgments

The idea of writing this book came from working together in the Brand and Strategy Council for the Canadian Marketing Association. In the early days, Patricia McQuillan, President, Brand Matters Inc. and Sharon Groom, Partner, McMillan LLP, spent many hours with us developing ideas and the framework for the book. We would like to recognize their invaluable contribution.

We are also grateful to the family and friends who supported and encouraged us throughout this endeavour.

Front cover photography and graphics: Michael MacLaverty

Foreword

Why is Internal Branding more important than ever before?

With products becoming commoditized, price differentiation no longer sustainable and customers demanding more, companies now recognize the requirement to compete on the concept of customer experience.

A successful internal branding programme is the key to creating engaged and motivated employees and those employees are the most important asset in delivering the appropriate customer experience.

In fact, an Internal Branding programme literally acts as the bridge between business strategy and implementation.

About this workbook

This workbook is a practical, concise, "how to" on Internal Branding that can be used by organizations of any size to establish or revitalize their Internal Branding programme.

It starts from the basic question of "What is Internal Branding?" and moves on to assist companies in examining their own corporate personality, strategies and vision before continuing with concrete advice on implementation and sustainability.

Table of Contents

1	What are we talking about?	5
2	Why is it important?	13
3	Who is in charge?	25
4	What do we now have and where are we going?	35
5	How do we establish Values for Employees?	44
6	How do we translate Values into Behaviours?	55
7	What Stories do we tell?	65
8	How do we Implement?	73
9	What do we Measure?	84
10	Summary: So what did you get?	91
11	Action steps	93
12	Appendix A: Employee Survey	97
13	About the Authors	100

Chapter 1

What are we talking about?

In this chapter

> ➢ Business practices within Internal Branding programmes
>
> ➢ Examples of Internal Branding definitions
>
> ➢ Steps to building your customized definition

The words "Internal Branding" do not have to strike fear into the hearts of the readers of this guide. Most companies are already engaged in internal branding in one form or another, although they may not refer to it as such.

For instance, the following business practices constitute elements of internal branding:

- *Employee internal communications*

- *Intranet*

- *Development of communication creative*

- *Internal Branding measures*

- *Customer experience design*

- *Employee surveys*

- *Rewards and recognition*

- *Employee behaviours*

- *Recruitment practices*

- *Employee training*

- *Leadership practices*

- *New hire orientation*

In this workbook we want to help you pull these activities together under one umbrella and further develop and refine them to create an Internal Branding programme. You may have heard Internal Branding referred to as many things such as:

- *Internal Marketing*

- *Internal Brand Alignment*

- *Delivering the Brand*

- *Branding the Organization*

- *Employee Engagement*

- *Operationalizing the Brand*

- *Organizational Branding*

- *Organizational Culture*

- *Internal Communications*

- *Employer Branding*

However, we will keep it simple and call it "Internal Branding".

Whether you are initiating the development of an Internal Branding programme on your own or you have been asked by senior management to lead the development of such a programme, the first step in creating an Internal Branding programme is to *develop a definition* that fits your organization.

There are many diverse definitions available, some of which are reproduced below:

1. *"Internal Branding is the set of processes that align and empower employees to deliver the appropriate customer experience in a consistent fashion."*

2. *"Internal Branding is the bridge between business strategy and implementation."*

3. *"Internal Branding makes sure your employees, distributors, vendors and everyone else are delivering on your brand promise."*

4. *"Internal Branding is aligning all employees to enable them to deliver on the desired customer experience."*

5. *"Internal Branding is having a continuous process in place by which you ensure your employees understand the "who" and "why" behind your business proposition."*

6. *"Internal Branding represents the relationship between an organization's employee communication practices and its business performance."*

7. *"Internal branding is a company practice in which employees follow company values, to solve problems and make decisions internally, and deliver an appropriate customer experience externally."*

While there are many similarities in these definitions, each has a unique set of words and inferences that could lead to different actions.

For example:

- aligned employees vs. empowered employees
- bridge between business strategy and implementation

- relationship between business practices and business performance

- inclusion of external business partners and vendors

- solving internal problems as well as delivering appropriate customer experience

As can be seen from the above, there are a wide variety of possibilities in terms of finding an acceptable definition for your organization. Nevertheless, we would strongly recommend that the time and effort put into the activity of finding an appropriate definition for your organization will provide the foundation for the clarity of thought that is required to build organizational support and collaboration for the programme.

Warm-up with some Questions…instigate some thought

1. What business practices already exists in my company that sound like any of the definitions listed above?

2. Do you need more than one definition to motivate different constituents in your organization?

3. Are you familiar with your company's organizational chart?

4. How will you use your definition?

Spring into Action…develop and share a customized definition

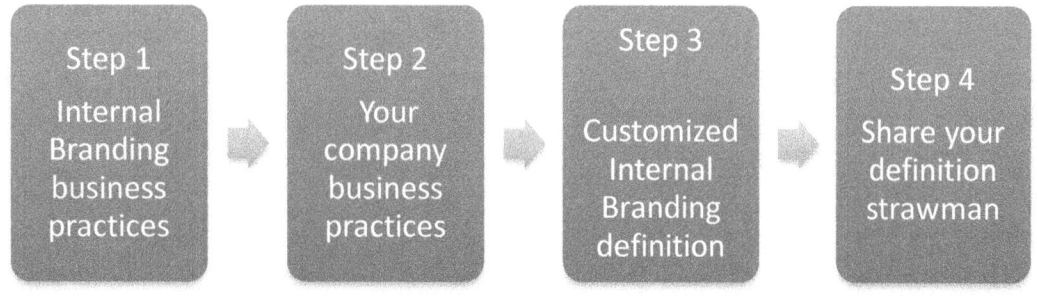

<u>Step 1</u>

Thinking about the examples of business practices, names and definitions in this chapter, write down what practices you think should be included in an Internal Branding programme. This step will help you write a concise definition.

Keep in mind that Internal Branding facilitates implementation of the business strategy and therefore do not include activities such as your company's mission, vision, business strategy development, financial plans and forecasting etc. in this step.

In chapter 4 we will discuss the use of mission, vision and business strategy as a foundation for building an Internal Branding programme.

Business Practices that should be included *Examples: employee communication, training, new hire orientation, etc.*

Divide the list developed in Step 1 into the two charts below; business practices that already exist in your organization and those that you expect will need to be implemented. In addition, indicate the person or function that currently administers the business practice or, in the case of a new activity, the potential administrator. This step will help define who will need to be involved in the future and will also ensure that all the appropriate business practices are included in your definition.

Business Practices that Currently Exist:

Business Practice *Example: employee communication*	Person/Department Responsible *Examples: Human Resources*

Business Practices that would need to be implemented:

Business Practice *Example: Employee Engagement Survey*	Potential Person or Department Responsible *Example: External Research Firm*

<u>Step 3</u>

Based on steps 1 and 2, write your definition "straw man" (see examples on page 2). This definition will provide the foundation needed for the steps in the next chapters.

Hint: Don't over-think the definition at this stage. There will be lots of opportunity in the future to discuss the final wording with your partners in this process. It may also come to light that you will need more than one definition based on the diversity within your organization

Definition "straw man"

<u>Step 4</u>

Share your definition "straw man" with the people you listed in Step 2. Adjust your definition with their input.

Definition

Output

A customized definition of Internal Branding that will resonate and motivate employees and senior management in your company.

Chapter 2

Why is it important?

"It is awfully important to know what is and what is not your business."

Gertrude Stein

"Pleasure in the job puts perfection in the work."

Aristotle

In this chapter

- ➤ Internal Branding's effect on financial performance
- ➤ Internal Branding; the bridge between business strategy and delivery
- ➤ Examples of how Internal Branding can affect primary business drivers of your company

---

Companies that practice Internal Branding perform better. From a tangible point of view it is becoming increasingly clear that those companies that pay attention to Internal Branding demonstrate considerably better financial performance over time.

This *bottom-line effect* should be sufficient in and of itself to convince senior management to pay attention to Internal Branding immediately and on how to execute it effectively rather than wondering if it is of consequence or not.

If we are prepared to accept that effective employee communication is a proxy for good Internal Branding then the recent Watson Wyatt study provides concrete evidence of the connection:

"Effective employee communication is a leading indicator of financial performance. Companies with the most effective employee communication programs provided a 91% total return to shareholders (TRS) from 2002 to 2006, compared with 62% for firms that communicated least effectively. Moreover a significant improvement in communication effectiveness is associated with a 15.7% increase in market value. Firms that communicate effectively are four times as likely to report high levels of employee engagement as firms that communicate less effectively."

Watson Wyatt "Secrets of top performers -2007/2008 ROI communication study

The logic for this correlation between Internal Branding and profitability is straightforward; to be successful a company must have a sound business strategy.

This business strategy is largely delivered by employees, whether they work in the back office or on the front line.

Therefore the strategy cannot be implemented unless the employees understand and believe in it.

The best way to communicate a business strategy to the employees is through an Internal Branding programme. Employees need to be motivated to live the internal brand.

The following chart illustrates that *Internal Communications*, *Employee Education*, and *Motivation of Employees*, are three steps key to improving the Customer Experience.

These three factors are a large part of effective Internal Branding.

Therefore, Internal Branding is *the bridge* between business strategy and delivery.

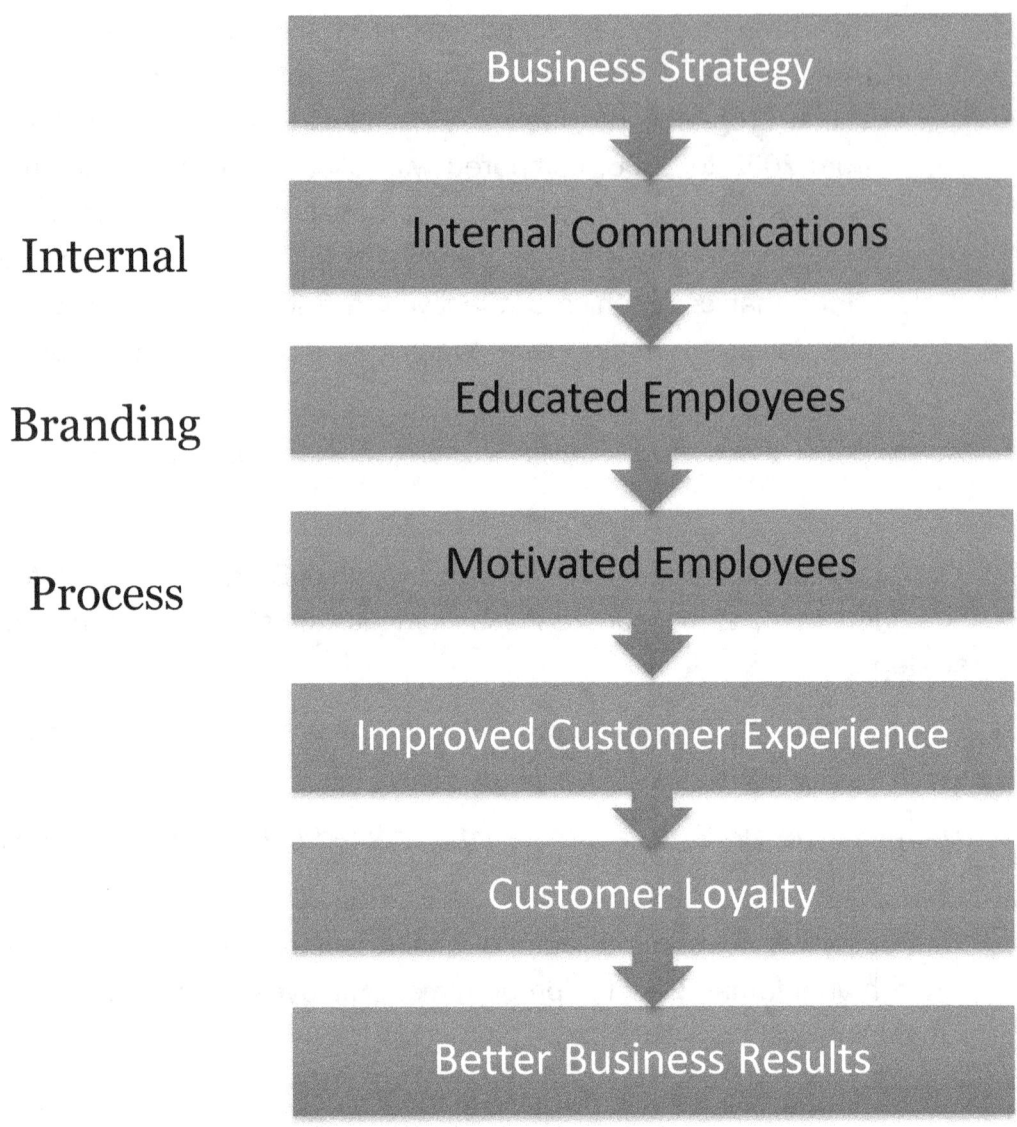

Internal

Branding

Process

Interestingly, it is not just senior management that is waking up to the importance of Internal Branding but employees are also becoming aware of its critical part in success.

In our 2006 survey* over 75% of marketers not involved in internal branding said "yes" when asked if internal branding was important to them as an employee, with the remaining 25% saying "sometimes".

*Internal Branding Best Practices Study, June 2007

This finding was re-affirmed with the 2010 CMA Internal Branding Survey.

This characteristic is not restricted to the realm of *business to customer*, it is just as relevant in the realm of *business to business*.

One of the primary reasons given by a steel company for its ability to continue to make money while the majority of its competitors went bankrupt, is because its employees from the shop floor up to senior management clearly understood and were able to deliver on the brand promise.

Furthermore, as employees become more connected directly with each other and indirectly with customers through the proliferating social media platforms, employees are embracing and recognizing the importance of Internal Branding. Social Media within the workplace will be discussed in more detail in Chapter 8, Implementation.

Successful Internal branding not only drives tangible direct business results but also, and perhaps more importantly in our view, it drives business success through less tangible forces.

When making a case for investing in an internal branding programme these primary business drivers should be recognized also. Primary business drivers are qualities in which a company must excel in order to implement a business strategy.

Five Examples of Business Drivers:

Let us take five examples of primary business drivers which may be relevant to your business: customer experience; attraction of key employees; retention of employees; customer satisfaction; and a company's agility, adaptability or speed of reaction to change.

Customer experience:

An Internal Branding programme enables employees to understand and have greater pride within their organisation. This in turn enables them to interact with customers in a more authentic fashion. Authenticity is one of the key characteristics that customers are now looking for in their experiences with providers of goods and services.

Attraction of suitable employees:

Use of Internal Branding as part of the "on boarding" process enables only those who feel a fit with the company to continue on to become full-time employees. This self-selection creates a more harmonious workforce. Greater cooperation leads to business efficiencies and innovation.

Retention of employees:

Internal Branding enables employees to forge a greater connection to the organization through a deeper understanding of mission, vision and values (business strategy). Improved employee retention reduces human resources costs with reduced recruitment and training costs. Lower employee turnover of course also has a direct effect on the bottom line.

Customer satisfaction:

Teaching employees the reason why the company has specific strategies and procedures enables front line employees to deal with customer questions more effectively. This results in fewer customer complaints, which in turn is normally a strong influencer of customer satisfaction.

Company agility:

In this fast changing world, if employees understand clearly the intent of a company, this enables them to be more focused and efficient. A workforce that is moving in unison with common purpose can be directed to overcome new challenges with better results.

These five examples demonstrate the way in which a powerful case can be made for an Internal Branding programme simply by selecting drivers that are important or crucial to your company and working out how such drivers can reinforce your company's ability to excel in these chosen areas.

More Examples of Business Drivers:

Additional examples of possible business drivers are listed below:

- Training and education

- Management commitment

- Customer satisfaction

- Staff Orientation

- Communication

- People - availability, skills and attitude

- Resources - People, equipment, etc.

- Innovation - ideas and development

- Marketing - supplier relation, customer satisfaction, etc.

- Operations - continuous improvement, quality

- Cost control.

Warm-up with some Questions…instigate some thought

What are the primary business drivers that are critical to the success of the company?

What is our most recent employee engagement measure? Is it above or below 70%?

Has our employee turnover increased or decrease in the past 2 years? What is the industry norm for this measure?

Do you know the cost to replace a manager at your organization?

What are your most recent customer satisfaction measures?

Is your market share increasing or decreasing?

What role do employees play in delivering the customer experience?

To what extent do competitors practice internal branding initiatives?

Are we able to establish a direct link between internal branding and bottom-line results?

Is engagement a Key Performance Indicator (KPI) for your organization?

Spring into Action...start to build your case for Internal Branding

The output of this chapter is the beginning of your case for implementation of an Internal Branding programme. As we mentioned in the first chapter, you may be initiating the development of an Internal Branding programme on your own, or you may have been asked by senior management to lead the development of such a programme. Either way, you will need a strong case to ensure enthusiastic support for and participation in your programme. For that reason, it is wise to connect your Internal Branding proposal with the business strategy.

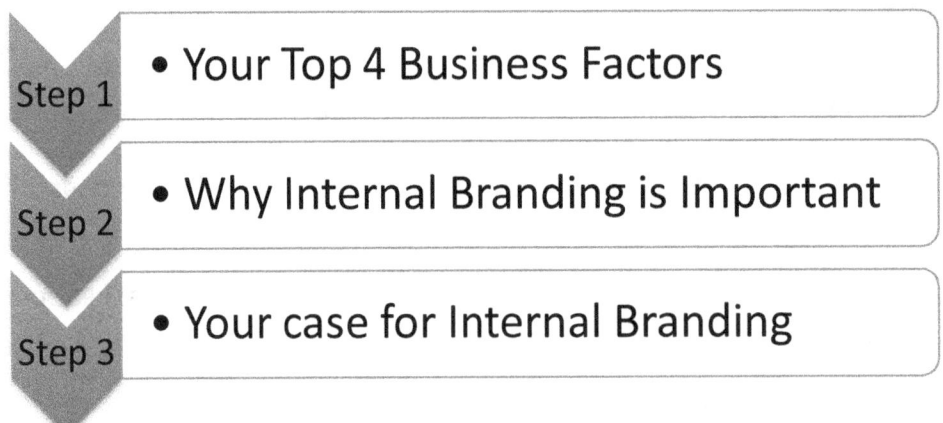

Step 1 • Your Top 4 Business Factors

Step 2 • Why Internal Branding is Important

Step 3 • Your case for Internal Branding

<u>Step 1</u>

In this chapter, we talked about and provided examples of the forces or business drivers that are important to the company's success.

Thinking about your own company, list the most important factors to ensure success in your business.

We will come back to these success factors later within the second activity in this chapter.

Hint: Don't over-think the factors at this stage. Remember that you are still in the initial stages of building your case and there will be lots of opportunity to verify the top business factors with a broader group later.

Top 4 factors that are most important to your business success
Examples: Customer Satisfaction, Internal Communication, Employee Retention etc.

Step 2

The second step connects the importance of Internal Branding to your identi-fied business success factors.

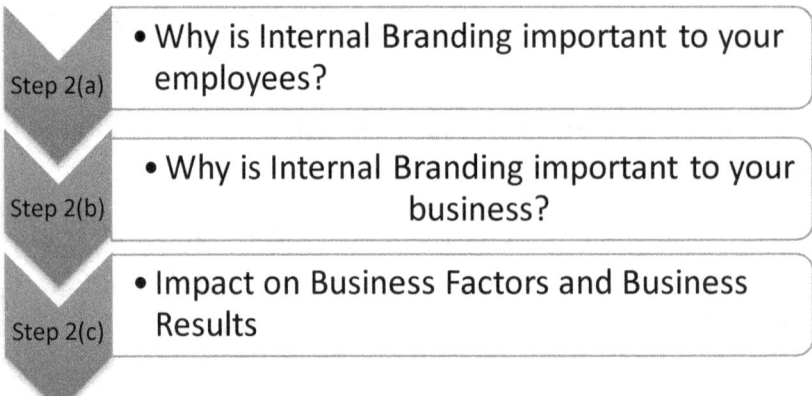

Step 2(a)
- Why is Internal Branding important to your employees?

Step 2(b)
- Why is Internal Branding important to your business?

Step 2(c)
- Impact on Business Factors and Business Results

Step 2(a)

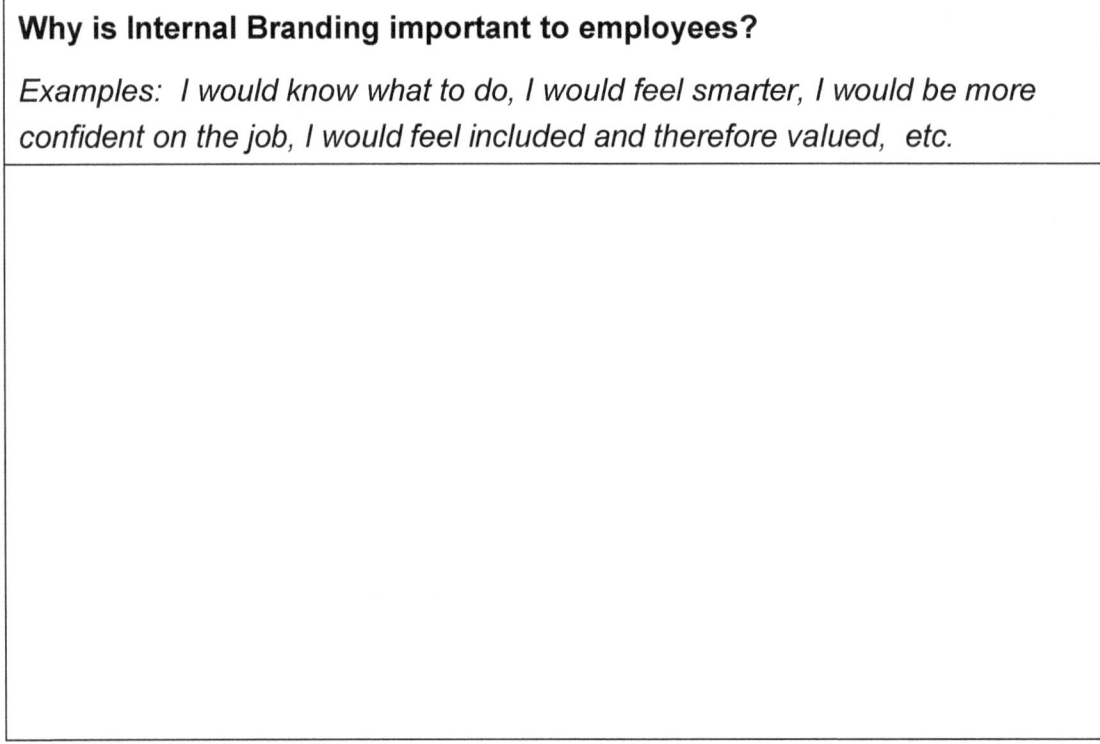

Why is Internal Branding important to employees?

Examples: I would know what to do, I would feel smarter, I would be more confident on the job, I would feel included and therefore valued, etc.

Step 2(b)

Take each of the points in step 2(a), edit or group as you see fit and insert in the left hand side of the chart below.

Next list the business result of your refined list in the right hand column.

Why is Internal Branding important to employees	Why is Internal Branding important to your business?
Example: • *I would know what to do, I would feel smarter* • *I would feel included, valued, proud of the company*	*Example:* • *Employees would understand how to look after customers* • *Employees would say positive things about the company*
• • • • • • • • • • • • • • • •	• • • • • • • • • • • • • • • •

Step 2(c)

Now that you have described the importance of Internal Branding to the business, let's connect that list with the top 4 business factors that you identified in Step 1. This will be helpful in building your case because you can precisely link employees to important business factors. While some of the linking may seem obvious, the more precise you can be in your case, the more likely you will engage your audience.

Top 4 factors that are most important to your business success	How "Importance of Internal Branding to your business" can support top 4 business factors
Example: Customer Satisfaction	*Example: Employees would understand how to look after customers*
1.	
2.	
3.	
4.	

Create your case.

Using the output from chapter 1 and the previous 2 steps from this chapter, *prepare and rehearse* for a meeting with your immediate supervisor.

We would suggest you include the work you have done so far in the following order:

Point	Logic
Impact on business results • Improvement of key business factors	Start with expected results to get attention
How – Internal Branding Programme • Definition from chapter 1	Explains Internal Branding, what is involved, who will need to participate
Why it is important to Employees. • Create statement or chart from step 2(a) in this chapter	Explains the importance of starting with employees
Why it is important to Business • Create statement or chart from step 2(b)	Explains the impact on business

Output

Sufficient argument to make a strong case for the Internal Branding initiative to proceed on financial and strategic grounds.

Chapter 3

Who is in charge?

"Effective leadership is putting first things first. Effective management is discipline, carrying it out."

Stephen Covey

"Management is doing things right; leadership is doing the right things."

Peter Drucker

In this chapter

➢ Importance of Leadership

➢ Forming a Cross Functional Team

We cannot stress enough the crucial need to have involved and committed leadership in an Internal Branding initiative.

In the previous chapter you built a strong case for implementing an Internal Branding programme. Given the expected business results, it really should not be difficult to convince leaders of the significance of their participation. We would go further and hope that the leadership would be a source of inspiration.

In addition to endorsing, facilitating and participating in the process, it is also incumbent upon leaders to demonstrate their commitment to the endeavour in their behaviour.

This is not always done.

For example, in our *Best Practice Study on Internal Branding* and follow-up research (2007 & 2010),

> *"only 22% of respondents in our survey strongly agreed with the statement "management walks the talk with respect to brand values."* i.e. more than three quarters of the people in our survey were not convinced that their senior management demonstrated the Internal Brand in their actions and behaviour. (More about values in the next chapter).

In the research, there was not a single company that had expressly dedicated an individual's responsibilities to "Internal Branding". More often than not, it was one of a laundry list of responsibilities in a marketing executive's mandate, parked alongside the responsibilities of advertising, branding, direct marketing, merchandising, etc.

One of the reasons for this lack of clear responsibility is the cross functional nature of the task itself. Internal Branding cannot be done by one person alone.

Internal Branding is something that breathes throughout the organization and it therefore makes sense that it should be originated and developed from across the organization.

The best way to achieve this, is through a cross functional team. A cross-functional team by its definition has representation from key areas throughout the company.

The membership of this team is important.

Members should be able to "voice" the values of the organization, and be well connected and respected in their own departments.

The team should have representation from as many diverse functions as is practicable without making the team unwieldy. Certainly, marketing, human resources, client contact, and operations might form the core of the representation.

One or Two Teams? Depending on the size and complexity of the organization, it may be desirable to have *two layers of team*: a small cadre of very senior executives at one level who provide guidance, decision-making and commands for implementation, and underneath a broader and larger team who are charged with originating and developing all the parts necessary for a successful internal brand initiative, as is outlined in the ensuing chapters of this book.

The team needs to be supported with clear ground rules in terms of the time, money and other resources that come with the initiative.

The exercises in this chapter provide further insight on how best to develop a cross functional team. Returning to leadership once more; it is essential for leadership to provide the team with a very clear mandate and set of expectations.

In conclusion, notwithstanding the paramount importance of an engaged, proactive and role-modeling leadership team, it is also incumbent on everyone within the organization to take a leadership stance, enacting the values and behaviours associated with the internal brand.

Warm-up with some Questions...instigate some thought

- Do you feel you have senior leadership support?

- Is there a key individual who is not on side with the initiative and if so what can be done to remedy the situation?

- Do you have the correct functions and people involved?

- Are the team members open-minded and motivated?

- Should you supplement the team with an outside consultant to keep the momentum and ensure an objective approach?

- What are the resources required to get started?

- What processes need to be put in place to ensure success?

Spring into Action…build the team and the plan

The following steps assume there has been a "go-ahead" by senior management based on the case developed in Chapter 2, Step 3.

Now that you have developed your company's definition of Internal Branding, and developed your business case it is time to prepare for and to form your team.

As mentioned in this chapter, the first step is to determine the structure of the group.

Will this be one team reporting to a project sponsor, or two layers of a team, one level for guidance and decision-making and a subordinate team for implementation?

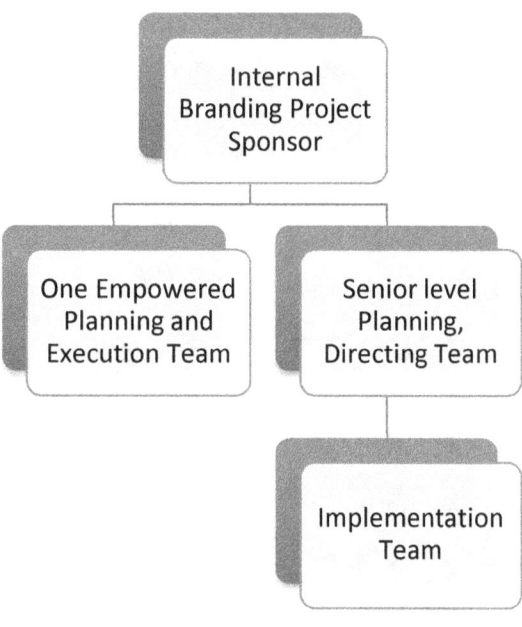

Regardless of the team structure, the project approach and tasks will be the same. For example:

- Discovery and education phase – Internal Branding literacy, leveraging existing company strategy

- Focus and approach – determining the best plan and the best implementation method to inspire your company

- Engagement description and project plan – detailed description of the work, timelines, budget etc.

- Reporting structure, updating sponsor, defined decision making

- Implementation and measurement

If there are two teams, the only difference will be to determine the tasks, authority, empowerment and mandate of each team. To simplify the exercises in this chapter, we have assumed there will only be one group.

Before the cross function team is formed you need to prepare for your first team meeting. The more knowledgeable and confident you are in the project, the more inspired your team will be.

There are four short steps for this preparation, all of which are easily developed from the previous work completed in chapters 1 and 2.

Before the team is formed

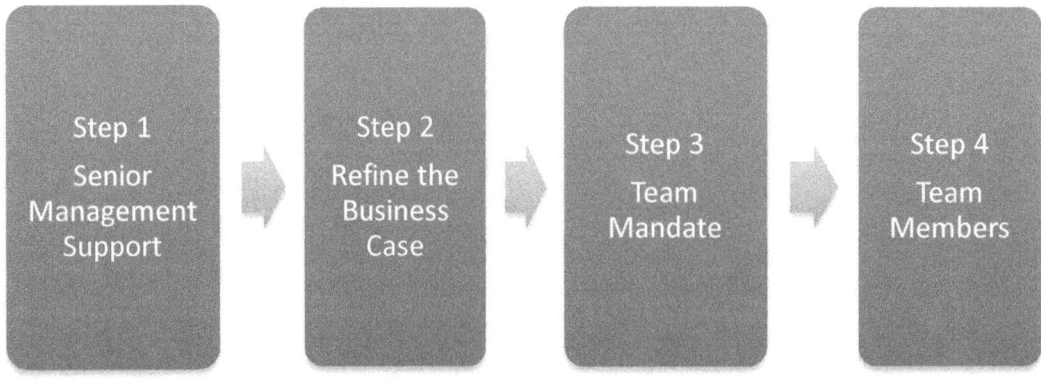

<u>After the team is formed</u>

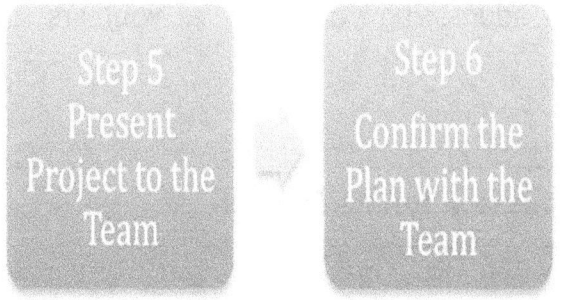

Step 1 – Senior Management Support

As mentioned at the beginning of this chapter, it is crucial that senior management are involved in and support your Internal Branding initiative.

Your first step is to acknowledge who, in the senior management team will be your best supporters.

The purpose of this step is to twofold:

- Top supporters can advocate on your behalf if you encounter roadblocks.

- Your team will have more confidence and enthusiasm if you assure them that senior management supports their work. Hopefully, you will be able to cite examples of conversations with senior management to substantiate your claim.

In addition to your top supporters, there may be individuals who do not support or are opposed to the project.

If so, ask for help or advice from your top supporters.

Try to book a short meeting with each manager, and confirm your first impressions.

Take notes and then list the discussion points and quotes from the Manager.

These notes will be helpful when addressing your team at your first team meeting.

Senior Manager Name	Discussion Points/Quotes
1.	
2.	
3.	

Step 2 – Refining your Business Case

This should be a relatively simple step and may not be required. In Chapter 2, your final step was to build a business case to present to senior management.

If there are no changes as a result of that meeting, simply insert your business case here and move on to step 3.

If some revisions are necessary, insert your edited version here.

Business Case for Internal Branding Initiative

Step 3 – Create a Draft Team Mandate

At this point in the process, you are simply framing the task to inform your team. If you have a format for projects that is currently used within your organization, use it.

Hint: Don't over-think the mandate at this stage. The first step for your team will be to edit your draft and create a new version. This is an important step for the team to ensure each member feels ownership to the initiative.

The draft mandate should include:

- Purpose and scope of the project

- Objectives, deliverables and timelines

- Description of the work, methods to be used to satisfy the objectives, budget, reporting, milestones etc.

Draft Internal Branding Team Mandate

Purpose	
Objectives	
Description of Project, Budget, Reporting Progress, Milestones	

Step 4 – Confirming Team Members

In Chapter 1, you built a customized definition of Internal Branding. Leading up to that output, in Step 2 you defined the potential person or department that needed to be involved with this initiative. Additionally, you may have had conversations with senior management regarding potential team members.

Armed with this information, create your team member list.

Department or Function within your company	Team Member's Name

Step 5 - Presenting the Project to the Team

You have all the material to build a compelling presentation to your newly formed team:

- A customized definition of Internal Branding from Chapter 1

- A business case that has been endorsed by Senior Management from Chapter 2

- A Team Mandate from this chapter

It is now time to book a meeting and present the project to the Team. You may want to have a Senior Manager introduce the subject and your role to the team.

Step 6 – Confirming the Project with the Team

In order to ensure ownership and enthusiasm for the project, you need to solicit feedback from the group and if it makes sense, alter the mandate to suit the group's requirements.

Depending on the group and your preference, you can do this with the entire group or break into smaller teams and have each report back to the group at large.

Note: You may decide that it is necessary to conduct a team building exercise with your group. This can be as simple as a coffee or lunch with the group offsite or as formal as a structured team-building meeting.

Output

Formation of an Internal Branding Cross Functional Team including:

- Defined corporate support

- Clear mandate and aligned goals

- Clear and understood methods of reporting progress, establishing milestones

Chapter 4

What do we have and where are we going?

Ancient Greek aphorism: Know Thyself

'Companies have to wake up to the fact that they are more than a product on a shelf. They're behavior as well.' - Robert Haas Of Levi Strauss

Customers long to interact with - even relate to - employees who act like there is still a light on inside. - Chip Bell

Our mission statement about treating people with respect and dignity is not just words but a creed we live by every day. You can't expect your employees to exceed the expectations of your customers if you don't exceed the employees' expectations of management. Howard Schultz, CEO Starbucks Coffee

In this chapter

> Gathering information from within your company

> Examples of Mission and Vision Statements

> Linking existing company information to Internal Branding

Resting under dusty piles of the latest presentations or buried in a sub, sub file, in a little used electronic folder one can find wonderful work completed by earlier generations of personnel.

For example vision-determining exercises are usually in depth and multifaceted rich documents. However, they are often only communicated in one blitz and then fall into the deep recesses of files.

Without a living vision the company will die; no purpose, no point. All the materials associated with the visioning exercise are likely to be very helpful in an internal branding initiative.

If one understands the "purpose" the "why" of a company, then all the things we do in it can be looked at through this filter.

Every activity can be evaluated in the light of how supportive or otherwise it is of the vision.

The visioning gives us a picture of that far away point where we believe an effective internal branding initiative will bear us.

Similarly documents surrounding "the Mission" of a company can be useful in an internal branding initiative.

A mission, which tells us how we will reach the vision, provides direct input into the sorts of physical behaviours that are expected of employees which are required to achieve the vision.

Above all though, we believe that the values of a company are the most relevant in order to design and execute powerful and successful internal branding.

The values can be likened to the DNA of the company, crucial for carrying it forward.

For this reason the whole of the following chapter is devoted to values.

To sum up with an example; if the vision is 'to go to heaven', then the mission is to 'live in a God-fearing way' and the chosen values might be ' kindness',' humility', and' servitude'.

If one had clear documentation around all of these elements then the design of an internal branding programme would be greatly facilitated.

Examples of Mission and Vision

Company	Vision – what you want to become	Mission – purpose of your business, how you will reach the vision
Google	Google's vision is to develop a perfect search engine.	Google's mission is to organize the world's information and make it universally accessible and useful.
Canadian Cancer Society	Creating a world where no Canadian fears cancer.	The Canadian Cancer Society is a national, community-based organization of volunteers whose mission is the eradication of cancer and the enhancement of the quality of life of people living with cancer.

There are likely to be other sources of information that will also be valuable in the creation of an internal branding programme; customer and employee research are examples.

Customer research should provide information on customers' perceptions of the company brand, characteristics that engender irritation or dissatisfaction, (these have to be mitigated or removed before a shift in customer attitude towards the company can be affected), utility of the products or services being delivered, etc.

Employee research should provide information on alignment with the company values, the level of engagement, effectiveness of communication and current understanding of the internal brand and behaviours associated with it.

One doesn't need to stop there; business goals, business model, market segmentation, product categories, competition analysis, strength and weakness analysis, can all be added to the mix at some stage in the process.

From our perspective if one can pull some of the more intangible elements within a Corporation, this is a rich source to feed an internal branding initiative. Pointers to corporate culture, myths and stories about the corporation, rituals and celebrations are all examples of these. (We will discuss the important influence of stories in Chapter 7)

The ideal is to immerse the working team in all of this information so that they can start with a collective and in-depth understanding of the company, its history, present state and aspirations.

There are additional benefits to examining and leveraging existing corporate information.

Your Internal Branding initiative is far more likely to appeal to the employees if it is grounded in the familiar language and direction that they recognize. This is not a "flavour-of- the-day" or "re-inventing the wheel" exercise. It is preparation for finding the inspirational words to describe the desired employee behaviour in order to deliver your brand promise. In the next chapter we will examine in more detail employee behaviour and corporate values.

Warm-up with some Questions…instigate some thought

1. Does your company have a Mission Statement? When was it last updated? How visible is it? How often is it referenced in day-to-day business activity?

2. Has your company developed a clear vision for the future? When was it last updated? How visible is it? How often is it referenced in day-to-day business activity?

3. Does your company have an annual planning process?

4. Does your company have a five year plan? A ten year plan? Who is aware of these and how are they communicated? How often are they revised?

5. Do you have an employee survey? Are there questions in the employee survey that ask about your mission and vision?

6. Do you have a customer survey?

7. Do you have a means of connecting customer research to employee research?

Spring into Action...gather more information

In the last chapter, you formed your team and had your initial meeting. Now it is time to put the team to work.

There are four recommended steps to get your team started:

Step 1	• Gathering Company Information
Step 2	• Understanding the Connection between Employees and Business Strategy
Step 3	• Assessing the Quality and Value of your Company's Information
Step 4	• Competencies and Behaviours that are Currently Rewarded and/or Encouraged in your Company

Step 1 – Gathering Existing Company Information

As mentioned earlier in this chapter, there are many sources of information that will be helpful in building your Internal Branding Programme.

Have a short brainstorming session with your team to create your list of available information.

Existing Company Information

(examples: Mission and Vision Statements, business plans, customer research, employee surveys etc. Make sure all areas of the company are included in your list)

Assign each team member a portion of the list and ask them to read their assigned document(s) and be prepared to describe the document contents to the rest of the group.

Step 2 – Understanding the Connection between Employees and Business Strategy

Now that you have gathered your company's information, it is time to acquire the skill to sort through the documents to find the right insights to build your Internal Branding programme. At this point you are simply building team knowledge about the required employee skills and behaviour to support business strategy.

Using the examples cited in this chapter, ask the team to describe employee behaviour that would be required support mission and vision statements.

Company	Vision – what you want to become	Mission – purpose of your business, how you will reach the vision	Needed skills & behaviour to achieve the Vision and Mission
Example	*To go to Heaven*	*Live in a God-fearing way*	*Kindness* *Humility* *Servitude*
Google	Google's vision is to develop a perfect search engine.	Google's mission is to organize the world's information and make it universally accessible and useful.	
Canadian Cancer Society	Creating a world where no Canadian fears cancer.	The Canadian Cancer Society is a national, community-based organization of volunteers whose mission is the eradication of cancer and the enhancement of the quality of life of people living with cancer.	

Step 3 Assessing Your Company Information

Now that you understand how you will be using company information, it is time to look at your Company Existing Information list from step 1 again but this time with fresh eyes.

Determine what has the potential to be useful and dispense with the rest.

Existing Company Information (from Step 1)	Keep	Discard

<u>Step 4 Competencies and behaviours that are currently encouraged and/or rewarded</u>

The last step in this chapter is to create a list and do an initial assessment of the employee behaviours that are rewarded and/or encouraged in your company.

Once you have the list, discuss with the team to determine if the behaviours support or impede the accomplishment of your business strategies.

Hint: Don't over think it at this stage, as there will be more work on employee behaviour in Chapter 6.

Rewarded and/or Encouraged Competencies and Behavior	Facilitate	Hinder

Output

- Foundation of information to develop your Internal Branding Programme
- Team education on connecting company strategy and employee behaviour

Chapter 5

How do we establish Values for Employees?

"It is not hard to make decisions when you know what your values are." Roy
Disney

In this chapter

- ➤ Definition and examples of values
- ➤ Process to uncover values
- ➤ Challenges in identifying values

How Do We Find Values?

In chapter 4 we likened the values to being the "DNA" that enables a company's culture to evolve. The evolution of a company is reflected out through its mission, vision and strategy. From this " DNA" grows all the crucial elements of brand, strategy, internal brand, behaviours, reward and recognition, etc. As with DNA, the process is iterative meaning that the mission and vision and strategy both determine and are determined by values.

Let us look at the process by which values are revealed or developed.

The process of uncovering values tends to be "extensive, expensive, and time consuming". There are 4-5 stages to the process.

The Core Development Team must include very senior management plus good cross-functional representation. (See chapter 3 where the formation of the cross-functional team is discussed).

Often an outside consultant is hired as expert or facilitator.

First stage - The Quest for Meaning

This involves competitive analysis, external research and best practices, re-visiting internal research, mapping employees' experiences, focus groups with employees and sometimes clients, non-clients, and suppliers, looking at myths and stories within the company. Local teams can often represent different geographic functions and specialties.

Questions asked in this stage:

"Who are we?"

"What do we stand for?"

"What do we do?"

"How do we operate?"

"What should guide our behaviour?"

"What do we want to be when we are successful?"

"How are we different from our competition?"

"What do we want people to remember us for?"

They are deceptively simple, clarity of responses to these questions are crucial and difficult to achieve.

Second stage - Distillation to the Ideal

Also iterative: different attributes and interpretations are often taken back to constituent groups for testing for applicability and accuracy.

Slowly, by constantly brainstorming, challenging, discussing, refining, and clarifying meaning, a set of values becomes forged; a string of corporate DNA laid out for all to appreciate.

Third stage - Relationship to the Brand and Corporation

This involves development and alignment of values into themes that are then put through the corporate brand filter.

Asked here are the following questions:

"Should the internal and external values be the same?"

"Should they be the same but a little different?"

"Should they be completely different from the values associated with the corporate brand?"

Fourth stage - Prioritization and Communication

(See Chapter 8 on Implementation)

This involves the development of key drivers and metrics and the identification of gaps between best practices and internal practices. Final polishing and development of concrete behaviours to be associated with the values, the on-going communication messaging and channels, the implementation of measurement process, the rollout plan.

Fifth stage - Going Forward

(See Chapter 8, Implementation and Chapter 9, Measurement)

This involves the development of maintenance programmes and ways to keep values fresh and relevant.

Examples of Values Adopted of Other Corporations

All companies that participated in some informal research emphasize the paramount importance of the role that values play in their internal brand.

Here is a list to illustrate the nature of these ``values`` taken from a half a dozen of our respondents:

- *Client Passion*

- *Creativity*

- *Accountability x 2**

- *Enthusiasm x 2**

- *Excellence x 2**

- *Caring Team Work x 3**

- *Service x 3**

- *Quality*

- *Innovation*

- *Integrity x 5**

- *Spirit*

- *Insight*

- *Respect x 2**

- *Commitment*

- *Responsibility*

- *Diversity*

*Number of times it occurred in our sample

The Challenge in Identifying Values

The subject of brand values is not as straightforward as might initially be thought. Some of these values can only be comfortably applied to internal branding – 'team work', or 'diversity' for example, and others have a greater application to the external brand promise – 'service' or 'responsibility' as examples.

Response to this dichotomy amongst the companies we interviewed was mixed. Some explicitly acknowledged it, and had two separate lists of values; one for application internally and one associated with the public corporate brand.

Others deliberately chose values that had both internal and external application so that they could have just one list and yet others tended to 'fudge' the issue including both types in one list and relying on appropriate interpretation.

Most companies' lists of values were short; almost all had fewer than six encapsulating words.

It is not just the words themselves that are important but also the meaning and nuances ascribed to them in the context of the company (e.g. "responsible" in one context means "we obey the law" and in another means "we will ensure our customer uses our products in a careful manner"; and in a third it means "we must make a sound profit for our stockholders").

Clarity around meaning for all has to be achieved.

For the international companies in our research, there were translations that were adapted to fit the local environments.

Warm-up with some Questions…instigate some thought

1. Should values be ranked or prioritized?

2. Are we missing elements from our research (e.g. external validation)? Are all stakeholders included?

3. Do we have clear translations of our values? Are there any ambiguities?

4. Are our values different from other corporations? Why /why not?

5. Is it important that company values be aligned with personal values? To what extent are our values aligned with employees personal values? How should one uncover employee personal values? Are all employees' personal values relevant?

6. In what way are values determined by the mission, vision and strategy and in what way do they determine the mission, vision and strategy?

Spring into Action…discover your company values (to the extent that they do not already exist)

The following steps cover the first three stages of uncovering corporate values as explained in this chapter:

Stage 1 – Quest for meaning

Stage 2 – Distillation to the ideal

Stage 3 – Relationship to the Brand and the Corporation

Stage 4 – Prioritization and Communication – Chapter 8

Stage 5 - Going Forward – Chapter 8 and 9

In the last chapter, you actually made a good start at understanding how to uncover your company's ideal values. Firstly, you examined and assessed your company strategy information. Secondly, you examined the employee behaviour that is currently rewarded and/or encouraged.

Now it's time to find the precise words that will enlighten and motivate your employees to deliver your corporate strategy and your brand promise.

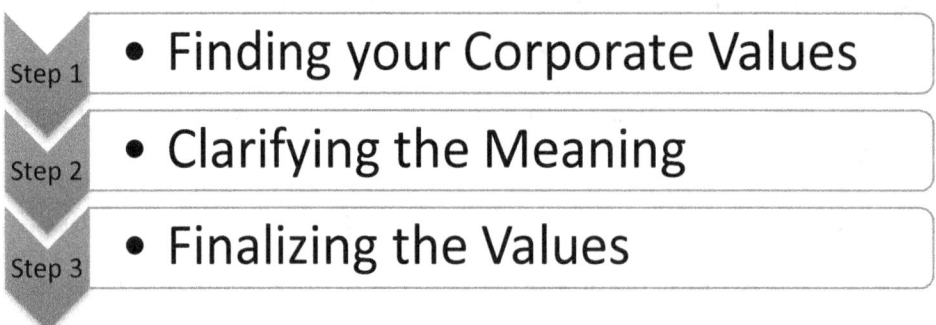

Step 1 • Finding your Corporate Values

Step 2 • Clarifying the Meaning

Step 3 • Finalizing the Values

Step 1 – Finding your Internal Branding Values

This first step expands upon the "First Stage – The Quest for Meaning" described in this chapter.

Review the questions asked on page 2 of this chapter as well as the business case you developed in Chapter 2, Step 2c.

This information will be the foundation for developing your initial list of Internal Branding Values.

Hint: This is only your first cut at a values list so don't over-think the values at this stage. You will be refining and editing the list in the next 3 steps.

Source of Information	Possible Corporate Value
Example: Google's vision is to develop a perfect search engine	• Creativity • Innovation

Step 2 – Clarify the Meaning of each Value

The second step requires creative thinking and brainstorming in order to ensure that each value will be clearly understood by employees. As stated earlier, it is not only the words themselves that are important but also the meaning and nuances ascribed to them in the context of the company.

In our previous step we used Google's vision as an example. Google's core values are actually ten statements with sufficient examples of each to ensure the intent is well understood.

Regardless of whether you decide to use single words or statements, whether you decide to have one internal and external values list or two, you will need to explore and test exactly what you mean by these words. For each value you developed in Step 1, write a statement or example of precisely what you mean. Consider even translating them into sensual representation e.g. sight, sound, touch, taste and smell.

Internal Branding Value	Statement or example for Clarity
Example: Google's statement for the value of integrity is "Do the right thing; don't be evil"	Example: Google's subtext for "Do the right thing; don't be evil" is: Honesty and integrity in all we do Our business practices are beyond reproach We make money by doing good things

Step 3 – Finalize the list

Now it is time to condense your list.

Most companies' lists of values are short, five to ten values.

Prioritize and edit your list, keeping only the values that will support the four factors that are most important to your business.

Often some values overlap and can be condensed into one all-embracing value.

Top Four Factors that are most Important to your Business Success	
You developed the four factors in Chapter 2, Step 2(c)	
1.	
2.	
3.	
4.	

Internal Brand Value	Clarification or Examples

Output

- Clearly articulated, easily understood, and readily acceptable declarations of company values.

- Supporting explanations and examples.

- An alignment between mission, vision, strategy and Internal Branding Values

- The basis for beginning the work to translate values into behaviours that will demonstrate them.

Chapter 6

How do we translate Values into Behaviours?

"Our problem is not to find better values but to be faithful to those we possess." John W. Gardner

In this chapter

- ➤ Relationship between values and employee behaviour
- ➤ Identifying employee behaviour
- ➤ Bringing employee behaviours to life through stories

In our previous chapter 5, we looked at how values were developed having noted that they were the DNA from which corporate life grows. In the exercises in chapter 5 we tried to make values a little more concrete.

In this chapter we go one step further namely to explore the crucial process of translating values into employee behaviours.

In chapter 2 where we discussed why internal branding is important we noted that it was through employee behaviours that the corporate and financial worth of internal branding are realised.

The majority of any customer experience which as we discussed in chapter 1 is now the vital essence of any brand, is manifested through employee behaviours.

When we undertake the translation of values into employee behaviours we need to make sure that the blinkers are off. There should be no limitations on the ways in which values can be expressed by the company.

Although we've noted in all of the previous chapters, employees are the main way in which values will be felt in the customer experience, it is imperative that such things as ambience, location, physical surroundings, noise, virtual presence, and all other environmental contributors are aligned with the manifestation of the internal brand and the desired customer experience.

Having said that, let us look more closely at how behaviours are guided and in particular the relationship between values and employee behaviour. For a start, all five stages of the process of revealing values outlined in the previous chapter will each have input into aspects of employee behaviour.

This leads us to the subject of behaviour identification.

Behaviour Identification

Most companies have some form of description of the desired behaviours necessary to deliver the brand which are in direct alignment with the brand values. However, these vary considerably in descriptive style, detail and length (e.g. one list included the following "Hand raiser not finger pointer", "Radiator not drain", "We not me", whereas others had the more formal "Everyone must be considered an individual", "We must constantly strive to reduce our costs" and "We act in an efficient and pragmatic way".)

All agree that behaviours have to be absolutely clear and preferably simple. For example, one company that had a high immigrant intake in the workforce might even use pictures by way of explanation of desired behaviours as much as possible.

Behaviours might consist of customer treatment protocols designed to deliver a consistent quality customer experience; while other behaviours might be outlined in more general descriptions of behaviours which could be applied to relationships both internally and externally.

There is uniform agreement that one of the most effective ways of communicating the desired behaviours is through stories, whether they be cases displayed in videos or print or telling the circumstances around a particular award, etc. Stories provided tangible evidence and context for behaviours that can be easily illustrated and remembered.

It is also universally understood that compensation, reward and recognition systems need to closely aligned with expected behaviours.

Warm-up with some Questions...instigate some thought

1. Each of the values implies a range of behaviours associated with the living of the values. What are the boundaries for behaviour at each extreme?

2. Do the behaviours differ for different clients/groups?

3. What principles can be identified that drive aligned behaviours that can be used as a base for developing reward and recognition mechanisms in the implementation phase? Specify them.

4. Should there be sanctions, remedial behaviour modification for behaviours that are misaligned with the values?

5. Should behaviours be different for internal and external stakeholders?

6. Should executives be given specific exercises to enable them to demonstrate brand values?

7. Should brand values affect decision making?

8. Have we performed a check-in to see that behaviours are aligned with mission and vision and strategy?

Spring into Action...turn your values into everyday behaviour

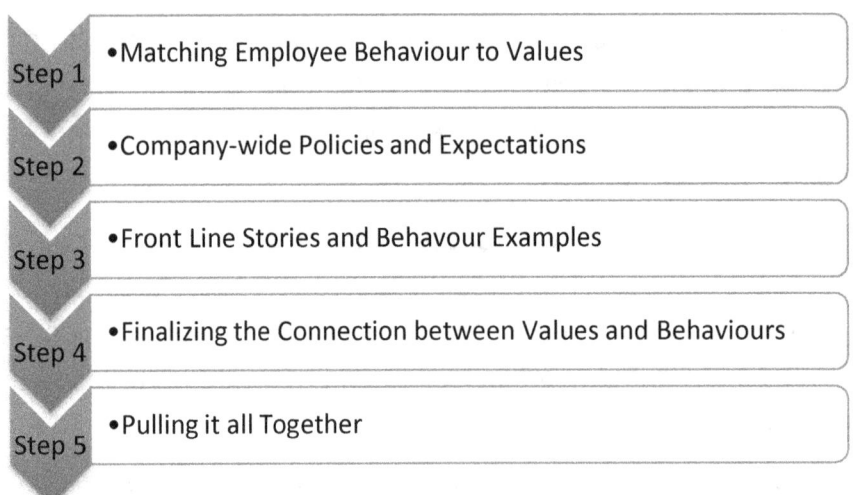

- Step 1: •Matching Employee Behaviour to Values
- Step 2: •Company-wide Policies and Expectations
- Step 3: •Front Line Stories and Behavour Examples
- Step 4: •Finalizing the Connection between Values and Behaviours
- Step 5: •Pulling it all Together

Step 1 - Matching Employee Behaviour to Values

List your company's Internal Branding values and identify the employee behaviour required to fulfill that value.

Your team practiced this theory in Chapter 4, Step 2 using Google and the Canadian Cancer Society as examples.

Now it is time to apply this theory to your Company's Internal Brand Values:

Internal Brand Value	Employee Behaviour Required to achieve the Brand Values

Step 2 – Company Wide Policies and Expectations

Match the Internal Brand Values to company policies and expectations; for example if it is company policy that stealing is an offence for which an employee will be dismissed, it may relate to honesty.

This step will be helpful to communicate the direct link between the Internal Brand Values and behaviour expectations.

Internal Brand Value	Company Wide Policy

Step 3 – Front Line Stories

Mystery-shop front line workers with deliberate challenges to the values. Look for examples of exceptionally superior behaviour and record that experience as a story.

Internal Brand Value	Front Line Examples

Step 4 – Finalize the Connection between Values and Behaviours

Armed with the information you have in the above steps, connect the employee behaviours to each of the Internal Brand Values. Edit and finalize your list.

Internal Brand Value	Finalised Employee Behaviours

Step 5 – Pulling it all Together

This step is optional but we would recommend drawing together a consolidated view of the work you have done up to this point; mission, vision, company strategy, values and expected employee behaviour. It will be an excellent blueprint for your work in the next chapter.

In Chapter 2, Step 1, you developed a list of the top 4 factors that are most important to your business.

Using those 4 factors or your company's strategic priorities as a foundation, verify that the Employee Behaviours developed will be instrumental in accomplishing your company goals.

Here is a suggested format to provide your consolidated view.

Mission and Vision

Business Success Factors or Strategic Priorities
1
2
3

Internal Branding Values
1
2
3
4

Employee Behaviour
1
2
3
4

Output

- A set of guiding principles for behaviours that are encouraged.

- A set of permissions empowering staff to behave in the desired fashion.

- Illustrations that can be used as guides for putting the corporate values into action and therefore creating the customer experience.

- A clear set of links between statements of mission, vision and strategy and the employee behaviours that will enact these (continuation of the output from chapter 5).

Chapter 7

What Stories do we tell?

"Stories are the single most powerful weapon in a leader's arsenal."

Howard Gardner, Harvard University

"Stories are the creative conversion of life itself into a more powerful, clearer, more meaningful experience. They are the currency of human contact."

Robert McKee

"Stories are how we learn. The progenitors of the world's religions understood this, handing down our great myths and legends from generation to generation."

Bill Mooney and David Holt, The Storyteller's Guide

"Good Management is largely a matter of love. Or if you are uncomfortable with that word, call it caring, because proper management involves caring for people not manipulating them." James Auty

In this chapter

- ➤ Translating the corporate vision into a meaningful stories
- ➤ Example of a company story
- ➤ Connecting the stories with individual roles in the company

---

In each of chapters three, four, five and six we have talked about the importance of stories and their place in illustrating the communication of the internal brand. As human beings, we love stories, and are well able to absorb information when presented in this format. Just before going into implementation, we believe it would be beneficial to look at and bring together stories at three levels, so that they can be continuously incorporated into all aspects of the implementation in the next chapter.

The three levels of story are:

- **The all-embracing Company story**. The story that is used to provide the raison d'être for being and growing.

- **The common cultural stories**. These stories of events, examples, myths etc. illustrate again and again the values and behaviours associated within and an alignment of vision and mission.

- Lastly, there are **the very personal stories**. Those stories that are true to you, the reader, that will help you, deliver the understanding of the internal brand from a powerful and personal perspective.

Company story:

Starting with the first level of story – the all-embracing Company story. All good stories have a beginning, a middle, and an end.

For companies, they are often in the format of, "where have we come from?" "where are we now?"; and "where will we be in the future?". In the same way, our information so far gathered, can be put into this framework.

It is the story of the company, put into the context of, or looking through glasses of, the internal brand.

As an example, or if you will "a case study", of what we mean, here follows a fictional company's story that may illustrate some of the key points that might be relevant or stimulate thinking for the creation of our own company's story:

A long time ago, there was a man in a rural village who was a skilled carpenter and designer. He built a lot of his own furniture for his own house. The furniture was made exclusively from wood that came from indigenous trees. A unique feature of the wood he used was the beau-

tiful grain and patterning to be found in it. Furthermore, it was all sourced from naturally sustainable, local, forests.

His neighbours admired his furniture very much and often when they rendered him a service of their own, they would ask him to pay them by making a piece of furniture for them - a barter trade was established. Each piece was, of course, unique due to the very nature of the patterning in the wood.

Soon people were asking if they could buy his furniture for presents and for their own use. His business began to grow rapidly. His two sons started to help him, learning his techniques which were often derived from old craft practices of earlier centuries. He would exhibit at the local craft shows and sales were good.

Now he employs nearly 20 people, mostly part-time and from the villages nearby.

Much of his employment criteria are oriented to providing an income and support to families who might otherwise struggle to survive in such a remote, rural area where there are few jobs. Sustainability in all its facets might well be one of the core values. His line of furniture has expanded from just the dining room tables he used to produce, into occasional tables, chairs, coat racks, picture frames, to complex chests of drawers and down to simple wooden table coasters.

His vision is to grow the company sufficiently to support all of his family and simultaneously provide a positive economic force for the rural community in which he lives while remaining true to his original principles.

His work is attracting two sorts of customers; big chain retailers who are looking for large quantities of production furniture and upmarket individuals who are looking for creative, artistic and high quality pieces.

It is now an incorporated company and about to go through rapid change and expansion. The production pieces will be made by introducing some new manufacturing processes – using automated lathes *and sanders for example and the original owner and his sons will con-centrate more on the high-end value "art" pieces of furniture.*

The values of rigorously only using locally grown and sustainable tim-ber, having each piece as a "one-of-a-kind", supporting the local com-munity employment, maintaining differentiation by uniqueness of design, must be inherent and guide any initiatives to increase produc-tion. Some new practices, such as the introduction of barcodes for each piece, have to be brought into the production chain.

But, overall the values of the original business are inherent in the whole operation and known by all.

This doesn't mean that all their business problems are solved. For ex-ample, should the "high end" pieces be marketed under a separate brand, or should there be an "umbrella" brand within which both the "artistic" and "production" pieces would be marketed in the same fo-rum? What would you advise?

The owner tells this story, from humble beginnings to complex production, over and over again, to all his customers and suppliers.

He is sure to emphasise the values with which he started and which still guide him now. He lives and embodies them.

His employees all know the history of the company and would tell you the same tale, in their own words, if asked.

It is now incumbent upon you to write your own real live equivalent for *your* company to which any audience within it would immediately relate. This, accompanied by the business case and related materials, should be sufficient to provide the foundation for the launch into implementation.

Once this story has been developed and agreed, it can be used to inform the whole implementation process.

The implementation process simply becomes an extension and integral part of the whole company story.

When combined with the business case it is a powerful way to capture the buying in of the whole of the senior management team.

Common cultural story:

The gathering of the second level stories should largely have been completed within the activities of earlier chapters. The legends and examples that are a powerful element in illustrating the culture of the company and its brand values should be collected in one place.

An example of these sorts of stories is to be found in FedEx. Stories of delivery personnel fighting their way through snowdrifts to ensure delivery; the extraordinary and efforts that an individual took to get a wedding dress to the correct individual immediately before the wedding took place etc., are renowned even outside the company and have featured in their own advertising.

Personal story:

The third level story is yours. It is not just the leadership, but as noted in chapter 3, it is incumbent upon everyone to take leadership position when it comes to enacting and promulgating the internal brand.

The leaders of the company will have their own personal stories as well as the cultural stories which they will bring with them throughout the implementation process.

Now it is your turn, for you to you to develop your own examples and stories from your personal perspective to be used similarly.

Warm-up with some Questions...instigate some thought

1. Did you have enough information to write compelling stories?

2. Are there individuals in your organization that are particularly good at telling stories?

3. Do you have a story that every individual can easily relate to for each one of the values and behaviours you have developed?

4. Do your stories tell the truth?

Spring into Action...gather more information

At this stage, you are simply compiling stories that will enhance the explanation of each value and the behaviour expected by every employee.

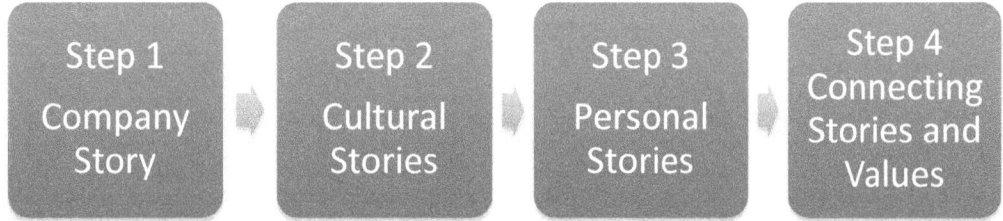

Step 1 - Company Story

This generally comes from the history of the company and its mission.

Step 2 - Cultural Stories

This step was started in Chapter 6, step 2. Hopefully, the mystery shops revealed some examples of exceptional employee behaviour and those examples can be turned into an inspiring story. Your task is to create a menu of stories from internal research, at least one for each of the values.

Step 3 - Personal Stories

Thinking about your personal experience with your company, create a menu of stories, at least one for each of the values.

<u>Step 4 – Connecting Stories and Values</u>

This step is optional. However you may want to create a table listing each value and the story or stories that best explain and personalize the meaning of each value.

Output

Your corporate story and a menu of stories that amplify the meaning of the values and desired employee behaviour.

Chapter 8

How do we Implement?

"In theory, there is no difference between theory and practice. But in practice, there is." Yogi Berra

"A good idea is about ten percent and implementation, hard work, and luck are 90 percent." Guy Kawasaki

"The value in idea lies in the using of it." Thomas Alva Edison

In this chapter

> ➢ Communication

> ➢ Reward and Recognition

> ➢ Recruitment

> ➢ Leadership

> ➢ Customer Experience

> ➢ Sustainability

In the previous chapter we took stock of where our journey in the land of internal brand had taken us, summarised the same and checked in with senior management, if necessary, to see that we were all on the same page. All the building blocks ultimately led to the creation of a set of desired human behaviours and simultaneously a clear outline of the customer experience we wish to impart.

Now we move to implementation.

No matter how diligent our work has been to reach this point, it is only through immaculate implementation that our efforts will be fully realised. For this reason, this is the longest chapter in this book, so strongly do we believe in its importance.

The first part of this chapter will cover how to implement tactics and actions that should engender the requisite employee behaviours; the last section will discuss some of the environmental and physical aspects of the customer experience and the influence of internal brand.

Essentially there are five major influences on employee behaviour and we will discuss the implementation aspects of each one in turn:

- Communication
- Reward and recognition
- Recruitment and training
- Leadership
- Resources

Communication

Communication is not implementation. Communication is only part of implementation; often it is believed that if everything is communicated well, then somehow nothing more needs to be done. It is true that without clear communication, most of the other aspects of implementation will fall apart, but it is not in and of itself sufficient.

Let us look at some of the other things that communication is not:

Communication is not just information. Clearly information is part of communication but the real challenge is to identify the changes in behaviour you wish to achieve.

Communication is not top down. A dialogue needs to be created with clear feedback loops and the monitoring of how people are responding. Social media platforms could provide a suitable medium for this dialogue.

Communication is not just one event. One needs to repeat the message over and over again and therefore an idea of timeline, frequency and channels used, should be in place.

Communication is not just one context. One needs to be sensitive to all the different contexts and what is relevant for each of the parties in different areas.

In order to be able to adjust and modify communication so as to be sensitive to different contexts, it is useful to understand the elements of communication. There are two fundamental elements, the message, and the medium.

The 3 Questions: In the context of an internal branding communication, three questions almost always need to be answered in the message:

- why the change?
- what is in it for me?
- what do I do differently?

Often, employees will first need to hear the message "you are safe" before they will be able to hear any other part of the message concerning change. Attention needs to be paid to tone, vocabulary, relevance, and length etc. of the messages.

There are a plethora of media out there today. Each adds its own timbre to the message. Care must be taken to match the message with the medium and an awareness of the influence that the chosen medium has on the message. For example, paper communications tend to be good for facts, videos are good for stories, staff meetings/radio are good for announcements. Each vehicle -- newsletter, television, social media, e-mail, face to face, video, song, intranet, poster, web, memo etc. will have an influence on the message.

A third element in communication is a sensitivity to the audience. Some anticipation of how the audience will receive the communication should take place. Increasingly, communications are becoming two-way dialogues, and a preparedness to respond to feedback needs to be there. Potentially there are multiple audiences that each need to be addressed individually -- internal, external, known, unknown etc.

These days communication is swift. No longer do we wait for the distribution of the Company memo to reach the staff notice board. Intra-employee twitter is instantaneous. Feedback and reaction to initiatives can be garnered and adjustments made almost in real time. As we noted earlier, communication is not a one-time event. The message needs to be repeated again and again. Ideally there is a complete communication plan in place, stretching out into the future time covering all the messaging, through which media, and to what audiences.

Reward and recognition

Interestingly, wages or salaries are not rewards, they are entitlements, fairly owed, in exchange for hard work. A conundrum is that much of the expected hard work comes in the form of desired behaviours that will align with the internal brand.

How, then, do we, in addition, reward and recognise those same behaviours?

At one end of the spectrum there is no reward and recognition. An employee performs the job expected and is compensated with a set amount of money and that is the extent of the relationship; a night watchman for example.

At the other end of the spectrum is an employee who receives nothing unless certain tasks are performed; a purely commissioned salesperson for example. By in large, monetary rewards such as incentives or bonuses are more transient and less motivating than intangible rewards like recognition and rank. In Canada, rewards associated with space and place are particularly powerful; private office space or a specific title in the hierarchy are strong motivators. In the US, rewards associated with status and public recognition are powerful; being made a team leader or a society president for example. A whole battery of ways to reward and recognise employees needs to be created.

As we discussed in chapter 6 a comprehensive list of desired behaviours needs to be made with a rationale behind each of them. Then these need to have some specific mechanisms for reward and recognition to be attached to them. For example an ability to nominate peers or other colleagues in recognition for outstanding customer service.

Slowly, the whole culture of the organisation will evolve and become more aligned with the internal brand. Employees are likely to become more engaged, and we know that higher employee engagement tends to be associated with higher customer satisfaction; in turn this is a contributor to greater profitability.

Recruitment

If the intake into the employee pool is selected for alignment with the company values and brand qualities, then the work involved in establishing and maintaining a consistent internal brand becomes that much easier. There is truth in the old adage "hire for attitude and then train for skills". At the same time it is useful to have designed some elements of the internal brand into the orientation programme for all employees.

Taking this further, some of the best practice companies have elements of the internal brand built into all company training whether technical, operational or skill based.

One of the most powerful techniques of instilling the desired qualities of the internal brand into the behaviours of employees is through *the use of role-play exercises*.

It is in the recruitment and training of employees that human resources has a powerful and crucial function in instilling and promulgating internal brand within the Company.

Leadership

So foundational is the participation of senior leadership that we devoted the whole of an earlier chapter to it. In the implementation section we wish to reiterate that it is not sufficient for leadership only to present and preach the message of the internal brand that they need to be seen to be physically demonstrating it too. Both "say" and " do" are important.

To the extent possible, leadership needs to be seen living the internal brand in both formal and informal contexts.

A particularly useful tactic is to gather exemplifying stories as they travel through the different areas of the company and to tell them back into the organisation.

Getting leaders to commit to a series of activities that they themselves will undertake to perform; a schedule of "town hall" meetings oriented around the internal brand for example, and also having them commit to supervising a series of delegated tasks; organising print materials and website changes, oriented around the internal brand, as examples, is invaluable in the initial stages of implementation.

Resources

Perhaps the most crucial task above all else for leadership to effect, is the establishment of sufficient resources for implementation. This not only means a clearly identified monetary budget, but also the freeing up the time for people involved.

Helping to implement the internal brand needs to be part of key people's mandate.

Many best practice companies employ external resources to help implementation. For example, developing creative communication materials is often delegated to an ad agency which specialises in these areas. Such materials are central to helping ensure that messaging remains consistent across the company. Again like all communication, this is not a one-off effort. Resources need to be in place to support an implementation plan overtime.

Customer experience

The subject of necessary and appropriate resources leads us into the non-employees side of implementation. Resources need to be devoted to evolving all stages of the customer experience whether it be awareness, discovery, attraction, interaction, purchase, use, cultivation, and advocacy, so that they are aligned with, or at least don't contradict, the qualities of the internal brand.

A useful implementation technique is to create "customer experience maps" that map the customer's progress through all of these stages.

Every sensual aspect, where applicable, needs to be considered, touch, smells, sounds, sights, tastes, at each interaction point across all channels.

Several studies confirm that superior management of the customer experience resulted in better performance in market share, retention, profitability and customer satisfaction metrics.

Sustainability

Again and again in our work in this subject area, we found that many organizations had difficulty not in the initial implementation so much as being able to maintain the momentum for years out. We would recommend that plans be built out at least nine months in advance so that there is a continuous re-freshment of the requirements of the internal brand. Build initiatives so that the employees themselves create ways in which to keep the message going.

Closely aligned with sustainability is having training throughout the whole organization on what the internal brand stands for and how it can be applied. This is almost a prerequisite for success in the initiative.

It is appropriate that we should finish this crucial chapter on the subject of "metrics and measurement" -- it is the subject of the next chapter.

Introducing appropriate metrics is essentially an extension of implementation. However, given its importance and that it is a discipline unto itself, we have devoted the next chapter to cover the subject separately.

In our view having an internal brand without implementation, is merely having a dream; implementing stuff without having a clear internal brand guiding it, is merely passing time; implementation within the context of an internal brand is making a positive difference.

Warm-up with some Questions…instigate some thought

1. Does your company currently use formal project planning?

2. What resources do you think you will need to successfully implement your plan?

3. What barriers might you need to overcome in order to ensure successful implementation?

4. Does your team have sufficient knowledge and skill?

5. Do you need external consultation to ensure success?

6. Do you need a project manager?

Spring into Action... start the implementation process

In this chapter, there are no steps for continued learning. We recommend that you use your company's existing project/implementation plan process. If that does not exist in your company, there are many good examples of implementation processes to be found on the internet. Simply pick the one most compatible with your culture and adjust as you see fit.

Output

- Implementation Project Plan

Chapter 9

What do we Measure?

"What gets measured gets done." Peter F. Drucker

"Not everything that can be counted counts, and not everything that counts can be counted." Albert Einstein

"True genius resides in the capacity for evaluation of uncertain, hazardous, and conflicting information" Winston Churchill

"The only man who behaves sensibly is my tailor; he takes my measurements anew every time he sees me, while all the rest go on with their old measurements and expect me to fit them" George Bernard Shaw

"There are two possible outcomes: if the result confirms the hypothesis, then you've made a measurement. If the result is contrary to the hypothesis, then you've made a discovery." Enrico Fermi

In this chapter

➤ Internal and External Measurement

➤ Examples of Internal Branding Employee Questions

Why measure?

As we noted in the last chapter, one of the challenges of implementation is sustaining it, so that Internal Branding activities permeate the culture and behaviours of everyone on a continuous basis. Consistent and repeated measurements help solve this sustainability challenge enormously.

Furthermore, measurement informs everyone as to what is working and what might need adjustment.

Finally, the Watson Wyatt study sees measurement as a differentiator between high effectiveness companies and low effectiveness companies:

> "Measurement provides insight into what works and what doesn't. That insight helps companies build on successes and refine the quality of their employee communication programmes. While companies are starting to pay more attention to measurement, they still have a long way to go.

> Nearly half of the participants in our 2007/2008 study regularly measure employee behavioural change, and just over one-half measure to see if communication helps employees work more effectively.

> High-effectiveness companies are doing a better job in all aspects of measurement. They measure the impact of communication on such business metrics as the retention of critical talent, workforce productivity, employee engagement and business performance.

> Employee engagement and business performance ranked at the top of this list. High-effectiveness companies know their internal and external audiences, do their best to communicate with each group, and use both. These companies are nearly five times as likely as low-effectiveness companies to hold candid focus group sessions with employees. That being said, there is still room for improvement."

What to measure?

There is no magic bullet that can describe the best measurement system.

The optimal set of measures will vary according to the type of company, the market, the competition, the level of sophistication etc.

Here we outline some of the possible measures that may be appropriate for your particular circumstances.

Measurements can be broadly classified into "internal" and "external" measures.

External Measurements

Consumer Experience:

By far the greatest number of external measurements tend to be focused on the consumer. Given that one of the leading objectives of most businesses is to provide the consumer with a positive, differentiated and purposeful consumer experience, this would make sense.

Measurements can be taken at every stage of the consumer experience, from awareness, to the selection process, to initial purchase, to use and to disposal. Well-designed consumer satisfaction and consumer loyalty surveys tend to cover most of the aspects of the customer experience. They should certainly provide clues as to where improvements can be made.

In our experience it is necessary to identify and remove customer irritants in the consumer experience before the true nature of the desired brand experience can be heard and felt.

In addition, monitoring and fixing sources of consumer complaints is an often neglected but powerful source of information and a method for increasing consumer loyalty.

Business Performance:

Another set of external measurements are those oriented around business performance; sales, market share, media mentions etc. These provide an alternative perspective on the success or otherwise of brand strategy.

Internal Measurements

Internal measurements tend to provide more direct insight and feedback on the effectiveness and accomplishments of an Internal Brand programme.

Employee satisfaction/engagement surveys are standard in many companies today and provide an immediate picture of how strong and successful an internal brand programme is.

We would encourage some questions that are specifically focused towards the internal brand be included.

Some possible examples are:

- Is internal branding important to you as an employee?

- How do you hear about internal branding messages? -- Video, intra-net, newsletter, staff meetings, executive briefs, other.

- Do you know your company's brand values?

- Does management actively support you to behave in accordance with the brand values?

- Does management "walk the talk" with respect to brand values?

- To what extent are your personal values aligned with your company's values?

- Are you rewarded for behaving consistently with the brand values?

- Do your company's brand values help you make decisions when dealing with -- customers, suppliers, direct reports, peers, management?

- Do you believe in your company's brand values?

- What symbols are associated with your company's brand?

- What would you change about your company's internal branding initiatives?

In *Appendix A* we include a further set of questions that might lead you to design an appropriate employee survey.

In our view, the advent of instantaneous and ubiquitous Social Media Platforms will transform measurement.

The results of customer, employee and supplier behaviours or points of view will be able to be monitored, analysed and responded to in the moment. Furthermore, they will strongly enhance predictability.

Companies will need to organise themselves around this new capability. (For a good to understanding of this see "Evolve" by Hessie Jones and Daniel Newman).

No matter what questions you used to measure, it is vital to act upon the results. Just having the numbers is not enough.

Installing a systematic follow-up process to the results of measurement will greatly enable efforts to sustain the whole programme.

The follow-up process would best include a methodology for the participants being measured, to generate their own improvements and response to the metrics. In particular, designing exercises that are aligned and reinforce the values.

Tracking over several time periods allows the whole company to see trends happening in their business and in their delivery dynamics.

To this end, internal brand measures can usefully be included in the non-financial section of the scorecards for those individuals and companies that use a scorecard system.

At the least, internal brand metrics should be included in the normal performance measurement criteria used to evaluate employee performance.

We would hope that by continuously taking implementation further, refreshing all the initiatives on a regular basis and then measuring and tracking the results, that "being the internal brand" becomes the natural way to do business.

Warm-up with some Questions...instigate some thought

1. What measures do I have in place today?

2. What type of measure will have the most impact on sustaining the programme?

3. Can I use customers to provide measurements?

4. How can I use new technologies to provide me with statistics for measurement?

5. Is there an ideal frequency for certain types of measurement

Spring into Action...gather more information

In Chapter 4, you gathered information from within your company and hopefully uncovered existing customer and employee surveys.

If so, here are the recommended steps to leverage what you have and possibly add additional employee questions:

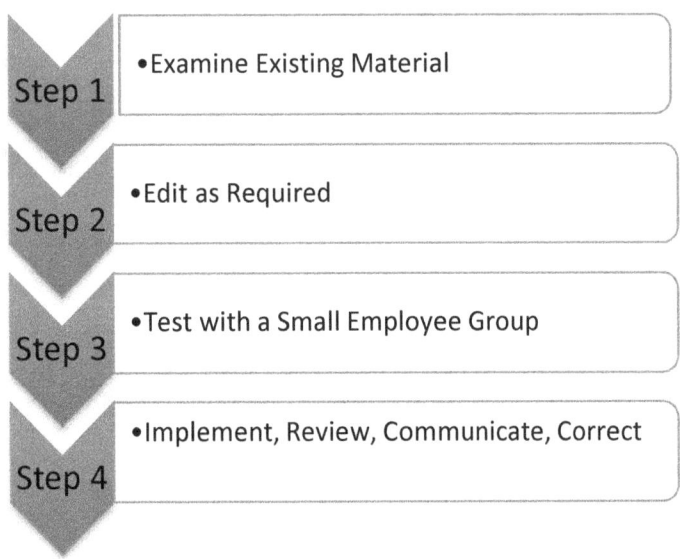

- Step 1
  - •Examine Existing Material
- Step 2
  - •Edit as Required
- Step 3
  - •Test with a Small Employee Group
- Step 4
  - •Implement, Review, Communicate, Correct

If not, we highly recommend developing an employee survey using the following similar steps:

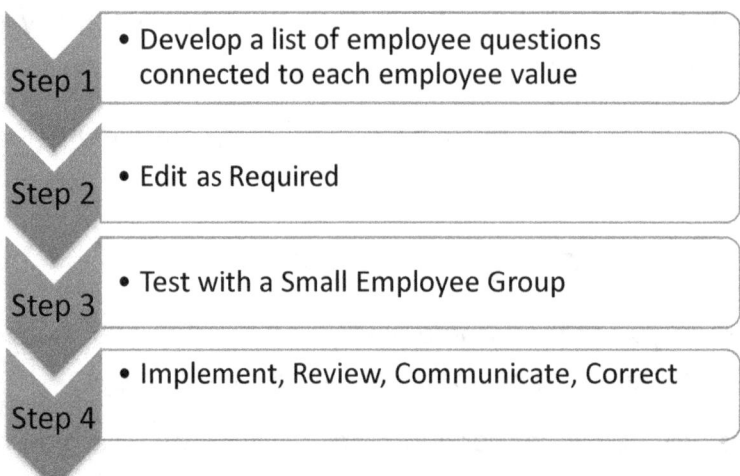

Step 1	• Develop a list of employee questions connected to each employee value
Step 2	• Edit as Required
Step 3	• Test with a Small Employee Group
Step 4	• Implement, Review, Communicate, Correct

Output

After reading this chapter and completing some of the exercises, you should be able to develop a comprehensive measurement plan using a combination of existing and new measures including:

- What to measure
- How to measure
- How to use the results for new or renewed initiatives
- How to improve or reinforce the values

Summary

So what did you get?

This is what this How-Guide gave you:

<u>Chapter 1 - What are we talking about?</u>

A personalized definition of Internal Branding that will resonate and motivate associates in your company

First step in enrolling senior leadership in this project

<u>Chapter 2 – Why is it Important?</u>

Compelling reasons why Internal Branding is not only important to your business but also to your employees

<u>Chapter 3 – Who is in charge?</u>

Formation of an Internal Branding cross functional team including mandate and goals

<u>Chapter 4 – What do we have already and where are we going?</u>

Connection of company strategy to employee behaviour

<u>Chapter 5 – How do we establish values for employees?</u>

Clearly articulated, easily understood, and readily acceptable declarations of company values with supporting explanations and examples

Chapter 6 – How do we translate values into behaviours?

Internal Branding strategic summary as well as a set of guiding principles for behaviours that are encouraged

Chapter 7 – What stories do we tell?

A series of company, cultural and personal stores that will amplify the meaning of the values and desired employee behaviour

Chapter 8 – How do implement?

Implementation project plan

Chapter 9 – What do we measure?

Comprehensive measurement plan

Action Steps

Chapter 1 – "What are we talking about?" Defining Internal Branding for your company

Step 1   List of business practices in general

Step 2   Business practices that currently exist in your company and person/department responsible Business practices that need to be implemented in your company and person/department responsible

Step 3   Draft definition of Internal Branding for your company

Step 4   Share the draft definition and adjust with their input

Chapter 2 – "Why is it Important?" Why is Internal Branding important and building your business case

1. Step 1   Top 4 factors that are most important to your business success

2. Step 2(a)   Why is Internal Branding important to employees

3. Step 2(b)   Why is Internal Branding important to your business – linking employee and business importance

4. Step 2(c)   Linking employee's actions to the top 4 factors that are most important to your business success

5. Step 3   Building your business case for Internal Branding

Chapter 3 – "Who is in Charge?" – obtaining senior management involvement and support, forming your cross-functional team

Step 1   Interviews with top 3 senior managers who you feel will best "walk the talk"

Step 2   Refining your business case (from chapter 2) based on interviews in step 1

Step 3   Create a draft team mandate

Step 4   Confirming the team members

Step 5   Present the project to the team

Step 6   Confirming the project with the team's input. Possibly a team building exercise

Chapter 4 – "What do we have and where are we going?" – Leveraging existing company information

Step 1   Gathering existing company information

Step 2   Learning how to find the right insights – using Google's and Canadian Cancer Society's vision and mission; list the required employee behaviour to achieve their vision and mission.

Step 3   Assess your company information – what will be useful and dispense with the rest

Step 4   Employee competencies and behaviour that is currently encouraged and/or rewarded

Chapter 5 – "How do we establish values for employees?"

Step 1   Finding your Corporate Values

Step 2   Clarify the Meaning

Step 3   Considering the top four factors that are most important to your business, finalize the value list

Chapter 6 – "How do we translate values into employee behaviour?"

Step 1   Take each Internal Branding value and identify the employee behaviour required to fulfill that value.

Step 2   Match the Internal Brand Values to company policies and expectations. This step will be helpful to communicate the direct link between the Internal Brand Values and behaviour expectations.

Step 3   Mystery-shop front line workers with deliberate challenges to the values. Look for examples of exceptionally superior behaviour and record that experience as a story.

Step 4   Armed with the information you have in the above steps, connect the employee behaviours to each of the Internal Brand Values.

Step 5   Pulling it all together. Creating and Internal Branding Strategic Summary

Chapter 7 – "What stories do we tell?" Creating your Company story to amplify the meaning of values and behaviour.

Step 1   Company Story from history, mission, values

Step 2   Cultural Stories - menu of stories from internal research, one for each of the values

Step 3   Personal Stories - menu of stories from your personal experience, one for each of the values

Step 4   Connecting the stories with the values

Chapter 8 – "How do we implement?" - communication, reward and recognition, recruitment, leadership, customer experience and sustainability.

There are no steps in this chapter, simply recommendations on the project and implementation process.

Chapter 9 – "What do we measure?" – internal and external measures, examples of Internal Branding employee questions.

Step 1   Examining existing employee survey material or developing a list of employee questions for a survey

Step 2   Edit the survey

Step 3   Testing the survey with small employee group

Step 4   Implement, review, communicate, correct

Appendix A

Employee Survey

There are innumerable questions which could be asked of employees and this appendix is merely to provoke thought and provide ideas in addition to those specifically oriented around internal branding provided in the text. (Chapter 9).

Response Rate:

A response rate in excess of 75% ideally needs to be generated.

A response rate of less than 50% is problematic.

Possible "engagement" measure:

1. "I am willing to go the extra mile…"
2. "The work environment encourages me to do my best…"
3. "I feel proud to be working for…"
4. "My attitude to working for… favourably influences my attitude to my job…"

The above four questions in combination are one possible measure of employee engagement.

A score of over 80 would suggest an engaged group of employees, a score of less than 60 would suggest a group of employees at risk. Analysis according to geography, tenure, age, function, and level would be some of the standard breakouts/cross tabulations.

Some alternative or additional questions for employee engagement could be:

"Every employee has the opportunity to contribute to the company's success..."

"My management/leadership team demonstrates (i) the values of the company, (ii) concern for the welfare of employees, (iii) a clear understanding of the strategy of the company, (iv) knowledge of the customer... etc."

"I would recommend... As an employer..."

"Given how I feel about....it would take a lot for me to leave this company..."

Other questions that cover the areas of:

Training:

"I have the knowledge, skills and abilities I need to (i) provide quality service/value to my customers, (ii) support other employees, (ii) demonstrate the company values,(iii) manage my job, (iv) grow within the company... Etc."

Work experience:

"To be effective in my job, I have the necessary: equipment/supplies/technology..."

"To be effective in my job I have the necessary assistance of co-workers/other functions..."

"My hours are fair..."

"The way work is distributed is reasonable..."

"I am paid appropriately for my job..."

"We work as a team to achieve our units/departments goals..."

"... is a fun place to work...."

"I receive the appropriate amount of communication to do my job well..."

Customer experience:

"In my unit/Department we provide our customers with the services/goods they want to buy…"

"In my unit/Department we consistently give our customers the attention they want…"

"In my unit/Department we record and resolve customer issues at the point of contact…"

"In my unit/Department we are recognised for exceeding our customers' needs and expectations…"

"In my unit/Department it is clearly communicated how we should behave with our colleagues and customers…"

"I have the knowledge/skills/resources to provide the customer experience that they desire…"

About the Authors

Nina MacLaverty

Nina has an extensive background in the retail industry including over 35 years at Sears Canada. There, she held a variety of positions throughout the organisation including Vice President of the Home and Hardlines Group and Group Vice President Consumer Marketing.

Her extensive merchandising and marketing background has given her a deep understanding of consumers and the retail and catalogue business.

Her marketing experience includes category marketing management, corporate promotional programme management and brand advertising strategy. She was responsible for corporate brand advertising, retail and catalogue advertising and in-store marketing, as well as leading the cross functional Group Vice President team with respect to marketing.

Nina also served as a member of CMA's Branding and Strategic Planning Council. Currently, Nina is retired and lives in Toronto, Canada.

Hugh Oddie

Hugh believes that only through embracing the abundance, embedded knowledge and skills of one's people can an enterprise truly recognise its potential.

Hugh is a master of facilitating new perspectives and opportunities drawn from the inherent richness already resident within an organisation. He creates wisdom at their frontiers. Hugh brings to bear three decades of diverse experience to his work. For ten years he was an Investment Banker. His career culminated as an Executive Director on the Board. Subsequently, he worked in Retail Banking for a similar period, at the head office marketing level in Canada's largest bank.

For the last decade, Hugh has taken his capabilities out into wider business arenas through consulting. He has brought innovation into the fields of finance, customer experience, transport, loyalty, brand, coaching start-up companies and personal development. Hugh was born and raised in Cambridge, England. He taught Economics and English literature in England, Spain and Mexico prior to his banking and marketing career. Hugh lives in Toronto, Canada. He writes poetry.

The Authors' previous related works

Published:

Nina MacLaverty, Hugh Oddie, Patricia MacQuillan, - "Internal Branding Best Practices Study", June 2007, CMA

Sharon Groom, Nina MacLaverty, Patricia MacQuillan, Hugh Oddie – "Internal Branding, A Human Resources Perspective", August 2008 CMA

Hugh Oddie – "CRM is not a Fading Fad", EFMA Newsletter

Hugh Oddie – "Why Loyalty Points Work Now and What is their Future", EFMA Newsletter

Hugh Oddie, Thelma Beam – "The Secret Life of Brands", Strategy Magazine

Hugh Oddie, - "The Carving of you"

Public Speaking - Each author is an accomplished speaker:

Nina MacLaverty has spoken on Branding at a CMA National Conference and two CMA Branding Conferences

Hugh Oddie has presented at the Corporate Executive Board, The Canadian Marketing Association and the International Credit Card Conference.